My Beatitudes

HOW TO BE HAPPY

by

Jean Webb

Spontaneous
Life
Publishing

ISBN: 978-1-7398954-5-7

Back cover illustration from the poem
"What if I were good enough"
spontaneouslife.net/poemsandprayers

Spontaneous
Life
Publishing

SpontaneousLife.net/Publishing

To anyone who's ever struggled with happiness.

*And to anyone who likes to challenge the established
view of things.*

Also by Jean Webb:

My Lord's Prayer (2022)

Contents

Introduction

How happy are you, really?

When you wake in the morning do you leap out of bed with a song in your heart and welcome the day with joyful anticipation? Do you jump enthusiastically from challenge to challenge with an ever-present smile and an ever-loving heart?

Or do you wake up and have to give yourself a pep talk before you can make yourself get out of bed? Do you trudge downstairs and start chalking up disappointments from the outset? Do you look at what you have in your diary for the day and groan inwardly, or outwardly, for that matter? Or do you feel a sense of rising panic at what is expected of you? Do your first interactions with other human beings lead to feelings of anxiety or irritation and annoyance?

Wouldn't it be great if the first scenario always applied.

I've come to the conclusion that one of the most important lessons we can learn in life is how to be happy. I don't mean in a narcissistic, pleasure-seeking way – what new ways can I find of making me feel good? I mean how can I find a way to a constant, true happiness? Something that enables me to cope better with life's difficulties, something to reach out for that can pull me out every time I fall into a rut.

Imagine if you had a secret formula for happiness, like a powerful anti-depressant that always worked and had zero side-effects. It would have to not only numb the pain of the bad times, it would have to allow you to thoroughly enjoy the good times – leave you with the full spectrum of wonderful experiences without limitation.

If you had a formula for happiness you wouldn't need to worry so much about the painful times. You'd just glide along and accept any struggles, knowing that you wouldn't be feeling pain for long, because you just have to refer back to the winning formula and everything will be good again.

And yet I do believe such a formula exists. I think that's what the Beatitudes are about.

I studied Ancient Greek many years ago, and recently started to use this knowledge to better understand the bible. I initially focused on the Lord's Prayer, then I kept feeling subtle prompts to look at the Beatitudes.

Is it just me, or do other people struggle with the opening line of the sermon in Matthew: "Blessed are the poor in spirit"[1]? I felt a deep dive into the Greek might help find a meaning that rings true for me.

I love the rebellious tone of the Beatitudes – the fact that Jesus is seeking to overturn the common thinking of the time. Now, in 2022, I wonder if there are things in modern life that Jesus would have us turn over?

---

[1] Matthew 5:3, translation common to many bible versions, as discussed later.

The Beatitudes

The word "beatitude" comes from the Latin "beatitudo" and means "supreme blessedness, or exalted happiness"[2]. It's the word traditionally used to describe the teachings of Jesus found in Matthew chapter 5 verses 2-12, and Luke chapter 6 verses 20-26, also known as the Sermon on the Mount.

Matthew has 9 "blessings" listed, Luke has 4. Luke also follows the "blessings" with "sorrows".

The following shows a list of the Beatitudes, according to the order in Matthew, with corresponding words from Luke. The version used is the New Living Translation.

Matthew	**Luke**
God blesses those who are poor and realize their need for him, for the Kingdom of Heaven is theirs.	God blesses you who are poor, for the Kingdom of God is yours.
God blesses those who mourn, for they will be comforted.	God blesses you who weep now, for in due time you will laugh.
God blesses those who are humble, for they will inherit the whole earth.	
God blesses those who hunger and thirst for justice, for they will be satisfied.	God blesses you who are hungry now, for you will be satisfied.
God blesses those who are merciful, for they will be shown mercy.	

---

[2] https://www.dictionary.com/browse/beatitude

Matthew

God blesses those whose hearts are pure, for they will see God.

God blesses those who work for peace, for they will be called the children of God.

God blesses those who are persecuted for doing right, for the Kingdom of Heaven is theirs.

God blesses you when people mock you and persecute you and lie about you and say all sorts of evil things against you because you are my followers. Be happy about it! Be very glad! For a great reward awaits you in heaven. And remember, the ancient prophets were persecuted in the same way.

Luke

What blessings await you when people hate you and exclude you and mock you and curse you as evil because you follow the Son of Man. When that happens, be happy! Yes, leap for joy! For a great reward awaits you in heaven. And remember, their ancestors treated the ancient prophets that same way.

What sorrow awaits you who are rich, for you have your only happiness now.

What sorrow awaits you who are fat and prosperous now, for a time of awful hunger awaits you.

What sorrow awaits you who laugh now, for your laughing will turn to mourning and sorrow.

What sorrow awaits you who are praised by the crowds, for their ancestors also praised false prophets.

Analysis

I make extensive use of the website biblehub.com for the original Greek, using the Nestle Greek New Testament 1904.

Unless otherwise stated, bible quotes in English are taken from the New Living Translation.

Since Matthew has the fuller list, I use Matthew's book as the basis for analysis. However, where both are on the same subject, I generally find it easier to refer Luke's words first.

My interpretation differs from every other version of the bible you'll find, but it works for me, and I hope you derive some merit from considering it.

Context

It's helpful to start with the context, so here are the verses leading up to the Beatitudes.

Matthew 5:1-2

"One day as he saw the crowds gathering, Jesus went up on the mountainside and sat down. His disciples gathered around him, and he began to teach them."

Luke 6:12-13 and 17-20 (first part)

"One day soon afterward Jesus went up on a mountain to pray, and he prayed to God all night. At daybreak he called together all of his disciples and chose twelve of them to be apostles. Here are their names:

<list of names follows>

When they came down from the mountain, the disciples stood with Jesus on a large, level area, surrounded by many of his followers and by the crowds. There were people from all over Judea and from Jerusalem and from as far north as the seacoasts of Tyre and Sidon. They had come to hear him and to be healed of their diseases; and those troubled by evil spirits were healed. Everyone tried to touch him, because healing power went out from him, and he healed everyone.

Then Jesus turned to his disciples and said…"

This section is often called the "Sermon on the mount", and both accounts mention a mountain. Matthew tells us that Jesus went up the mountain, with his disciples, and he spoke to them. Luke tells us that Jesus had been up a mountain and then came down, and was speaking on a large, level area.

There is speculation that the two accounts could be referring to different occasions. To me it makes no odds. If you go to see a singer or a comedian on tour you'll no doubt hear the same songs or the same jokes at multiple venues, but the essence, or the message, will be the same.

Both accounts agree that Jesus was focusing on his disciples. Both accounts refer to crowds also being present, so it sounds to me like Jesus could be referring to his disciples for the others to hear, using his disciples as examples.

Luke speaks in the second person, "the kingdom of God is yours" (Luke 6:20), whereas Matthew speaks in the third person, "theirs is the kingdom of heaven" (Matthew 5:3), presumably pointing in some way to the disciples.

The Disciples

If the disciples are, as I believe they are, the subject of the Beatitudes, it's perhaps worth understanding a little about them at this point.

We know that they left everything to follow Jesus:

> *Re Simon Peter and Andrew:* "And they left their nets and followed him." (Matthew 4:20)

> *Re James and John:* "They immediately followed him, leaving the boat and their father behind." (Matthew 4:22)

> "And as soon as they landed, they left everything and followed Jesus." (Luke 5:11)

> "So Levi got up, left everything, and followed him." (Luke 5:28)

They left absolutely everything: family, livelihood, friends, shelter, security, possessions, everything.

What would make someone a disciple, why would they have been chosen?

We know that they included several fishermen and a tax collector, so we can assume they had different backgrounds and experience.

Did Jesus go on a recruitment drive, looking for particular skills, selecting by some pre-defined criteria: people skills, resourcefulness, sense of direction, knowledge of the area, ability to control crowds?

Or did Jesus just bump into some random men and say "Fancy joining?" and they said yes?

We don't get any idea of why they were chosen. Did he simply pick on the first people he saw, being confident he could make disciples of them, or was he was looking for anything particular?

It's fair to assume that Jesus saw something in them, some kind of potential, an openness or a sense of adventure, a spark of interest, or zest for life, that made them right for the challenge he was suggesting. Whatever it was, he saw something in them that meant he knew they were right for the job. They wouldn't be perfect – who is? – but they would have to be keen.

Why would they have thought it acceptable to give up everything and follow Jesus? They must have had a very strong instinct that this was right for them. It's hard for me to imagine meeting someone I would trust so much so soon, but then, they had witnessed Jesus performing miracles.

If someone I knew came to me and told me they were going off to tour the country with someone they'd just met I'd be rather sceptical. If I had a son, who I was hoping would continue my family business, I'd take some convincing it was the right thing for them to do. If I had two sons and they both wanted to go, I'd be more than a little concerned.

What I think is reasonable to surmise is that the disciples must have had certain qualities. They had to have been courageous, though they may well have felt fear; trusting, though we know there were times of doubt; single-minded in their purpose; and they absolutely had to dismiss any concern of how their actions would be perceived by others.

The most important thing was that they were the kind of people who were prepared to say yes.

Blessed or Happy?

Matthew and Luke both use the same word throughout the beatitudes:

Μακάριοι

Makarioi

Makarioi is from the word "makar", and its longer form "makarios", which mean "blessed" or "happy". In this context it's almost universally translated to mean "blessed". I say almost, since the Good News Bible and Young's Literal Translation, at least, have it as "happy".

Let's think about who it refers to. It's an adjective, and is nominative, masculine, plural. (Further notes on grammar can be found in the appendix.)

We know from the context that Jesus was looking at the disciples as he spoke. This means the word describes them, and this fits the grammar, since they are the subject of the sentence (nominative), they are men (masculine), and there are many of them (plural).

There's an absence of verbs at the start of these verses, so there's no confirmation at this point of the fact that Jesus is addressing the disciples. There's no "Disciples, you are blessed/happy", nor is there "Disciples, they are blessed/happy", and there's nothing to suggest a generic statement "People are blessed/happy".

The second part of each of the verses is where we get Luke using the 2nd person – you – and Matthew using the 3rd person – they. My feeling is that the Beatitudes are about the disciples, for the benefit of the larger crowd. Luke is addressing them directly, Matthew is talking about them, but both accounts say that Jesus was looking at the disciples when he spoke.

The translation is generally taken to be "Blessed are the… (poor, etc)", which suggests that anyone who is poor, etc, is blessed, but that doesn't quite do it for me. I think it aids understanding to have the disciples firmly in mind.

I prefer to think of it as "You, disciples, are happy" (Luke), or "These disciples, they are happy" (Matthew).

Why do I prefer the word happy? Because Jesus knew his disciples and he knew they were happy.

I also think that, for passages such as this that we've all heard so many times, perhaps it helps to use a different word so that we challenge ourselves to think again about its meaning, rather than assuming we know what it means.

The disciples were blessed, no doubt, but I believe they were also happy.

How wonderful would it have been to spend your days following a man who was capable, at such an early stage of his ministry, of healing anyone who came to him. How wondrous must it have been to watch him and hear his transformational teachings? It's hard to imagine.

You can tell people they're blessed, but you can't really tell someone they're happy. There's always the chance they'll say "Actually I've got a really bad headache today, so, no, I don't feel happy at the moment" or similar. They might still agree that they are blessed, though.

Blessed or Happy?

What I like about the word "happy" is that happiness comes from within you, whereas the sense of "blessed" is that you've been in receipt of something that has come from outside.

"Blessed" may be a fact, but it's not necessarily a feeling. Happiness is the way it feels to be blessed.

Happiness makes you shine. Happiness bursts forth. It's like when you're newly in love and you can't stop smiling.

I think that's the kind of feeling that Jesus is referring to here.

Beggars

Luke 6:20 (second part)

> Μακάριοι οἱ πτωχοί, Ὅτι ὑμετέρα ἐστὶν ἡ βασιλεία τοῦ Θεοῦ.

> Makarioi hoi ptochoi, hoti hymetera estin he basileia tou Theou.

> Happy (are) the beggars, for yours is the kingdom of God

The first part of this sentence has neither noun nor verb, instead it has adjectives, makarioi and ptochoi, and a definite article, "the".

Makarioi, as I've said, is from the word that means "happy". The word ptochoi means "beggar". There is no verb, so literally it means "Happy the beggars". We know that happy and beggars refer to the same people as both are nominative masculine plural. We assume a verb, since our language is so less specific in terms of forms of nouns and adjectives, so we say "Happy are the beggars", and since we know from the next part that Luke is referring to the disciples, we could say "Happy are you beggars".

Beggars are poor in the sense of having literally nothing, being reliant on others for food, shelter, and anything else money can buy. We know that the disciples left everything behind them to follow Jesus, and that Jesus and his disciples were reliant on the kindness of strangers, receiving gifts of food and shelter as they went from place to place.

Beggars

Beggars are to be pitied, surely? How can they be happy?

The second part of the sentence explains why these beggars are happy, for (hoti) the kingdom (he basileia) of God (tou Theou) is (estin) yours (hymetera).

Here we have the formula for happiness. We have to own the kingdom of God.

Both Matthew and Luke use the word "kingdom" in this way, whether "of God" or "of the heavens", saying that the kingdom is "of you", or "of them", meaning the disciples.

What does it mean to say the kingdom of God is yours?

The kingdom of God belongs to God, surely? Isn't that what "of God" means? In what sense can something of God's also be something of mine? Does God agree to a shared-ownership arrangement with people of sufficient merit?

Does it mean to have access to God's kingdom – God has given you a key?

Perhaps it might be helpful to consider what the kingdom of God is. To me it is everything that is purely God, without the stuff that is human or in any way problematic.

Love, joy, harmony, ecstasy, beauty, peace. These things are what I would expect in God's kingdom, and therefore this is how I would define God's kingdom.

Let's try substituting these words in the phrase "the kingdom of God is yours": "love, joy, harmony, ecstasy, beauty, peace are yours". Now let's make it slightly more specific, because there could be other types of love and joy etc that aren't what we're referring to here: "God's love, joy, harmony, ecstasy, beauty, peace are yours". This I like better, but it's a bit of a mouthful. Let's pick a word that best sums up what we're talking about here.

God's love is what abounds in God's kingdom. However I think it would be misleading to say "Happy are you because you have God's love", as this would suggest some level of differentiation, that not everyone has God's love. We all have God's love. We might not be aware of it and we might not always feel it, but we all have God's love.

The word that I think best sums up what we mean when we talk of God's kingdom, particularly within the context of the beatitudes, is "peace".

The word "Peace" is used a lot in a religious context. "Peace be with you" is a phrase often used within church services. Many services end with a command to "Go in Peace and serve the Lord" or similar. Then there is the wish that's expressed towards anyone who's recently died "Rest in Peace".

Peace is what we strive for. Peace is the aim. When I get to the end of my days I want to achieve peace, I want to be "at peace".

Let's try this out:

> *Happy are you, beggars, because you have God's peace.*

Happiness Point 1: God's Peace

Here we have the first part of our formula. In order to be happy we need to have God's peace.

It sounds simple but what does it mean? First of all, what is peace?

Peace is the absence of conflict, it is the opposite of conflict. Conflict in any sense does not and cannot lead to peace. Conflict happens when we've tried to find a peaceful solution and failed, and the way to achieve peace after conflict is to go back and try again, only this time to try harder.

Peace needs forgiveness. If I don't feel at peace in my day to day life it's because I'm harbouring some negative thought towards something or someone. The only way to achieve peace is to identify that negative thought and either rationalise it away or replace it.

Peace is stillness, rest, calm, an absence of the turbulent ups and downs we experience in life.

I can spend a day at peace when I'm on my own, keeping my thoughts clear of anything that might distract or upset me, but then I realise I have no food and I need to go shopping. I get in my car, someone cuts in front of me at a junction and my sense of peace is challenged, I get stuck in traffic for a mile or so and my peace is challenged some more. The person in front of me in the shop takes the last on the shelf of the thing I most wanted to buy. The queues are long and ill-defined, someone who arrived after me cuts in front of me and they're buying loads more than me. When it comes to my turn at checkout there's a price missing and a long wait while the correct price is found. I try to make conversation with the person queuing behind me but I get a disinterested glare in return. I get back to my car and realise I've forgotten to buy something really important.

I arrive home flustered, annoyed, frustrated at the things that have gone wrong. I speak to my neighbour, I off-load some venom and vitriol a

bout the things that happened to me on my shopping expedition. They might share their stories of similar experiences and we share our hatred of going shopping.

However, if I instead choose the way of peace and forgiveness then I don't dwell on any negatives. I'll arrive home calm, accepting that it may have taken longer than expected, but nothing will have been lost. If I see my neighbour we'll have a cheery conversation, all smiles.

Peace is a choice.

Feelings that aren't peaceful emerge all the time. We each get triggered in different ways by different events. The more I can understand my reaction the more quickly I can return to peace.

Peace doesn't try. Peace is relaxed, peace is just "being".

The way of peace leads to happiness, it *is* happiness.

The way to own God's kingdom, or the kingdom of the heavens, is simply to seek a peaceful solution in all matters, all of the time.

What I need to understand is what my triggers are that form as blocks to peace, the better I can do that, the better I can return to peace.

Is Jesus saying that God's peace is only for beggars and those without material possessions? This brings to mind the "eye of a needle" comment (Mark 10:25 and Luke 18:25). Or does it mean that when you have God's peace you have no need of anything else?

I think it means that possessions, food, shelter, all our comforts, are of no consequence when we think of true happiness. True happiness cannot be found in money or possessions of any kind. If you have true happiness then you don't care whether you have these other things or not, they're just irrelevant.

Therefore the disciples, who own nothing and are reliant on the kindness of strangers, are happy regardless of this, or despite this, because they have something much better. They know all about God's peace and how to find it:

> *You are happy, despite being beggars, because you have God's peace.*

Poor in spirit?

Matthew's version is a little different.

Matthew 5:3

> Μακάριοι οἱ πτωχοὶ τῷ πνεύματι, ὅτι αὐτῶν ἐστιν ἡ βασιλεία τῶν οὐρανῶν.

> Makarioi hoi ptochoi to pneumati, hoti auton estin he basileia tin ouranon.

> Happy (are) the beggars in spirit, for theirs is the kingdom of the heavens.

In the first part of the sentence we have the same words as Luke, with one significant difference: "in spirit" (to pneumati).

This is usually translated as "Blessed are the poor in spirit" (New International Version, English Standard Version, King James, amongst many others). The New Living Translation gives us a different take on it: "God blesses those who are poor and realize their need for him", which takes us quite far from the original Greek.

I've always found this, of all the Beatitudes, to be the hardest to understand.

Bearing in mind that Jesus is referring to the disciples – are we to think they were poor in spirit? They would occasionally have been dispirited, we all are from time to time, but ptochoi is a strong word that means more than "a bit low", it means having nothing and needing to beg in order to stay alive.

However, one thing to know about Greek is that the order of the words as they are written is often not the order that works best when they are translated. One of the reasons Ancient Greek is so complicated is that quite often the words seem to have been put through a tumble dryer, so you have to match your socks depending on which are nominative, masculine and plural, or whatever.

The Greek of the bible is simpler in form than Ancient Greek, but still there are many instances of needing to change the order of the words to find the correct meaning, the best example in the Beatitudes being Luke 6:23 (see Appendix).

Could it be that, given the context, we should switch these words round? What if we put the words "in spirit" with "happy", instead of "beggars"?

"Happy in spirit are the beggars" makes a lot more sense to me. "In spirit" could apply equally to "the happy" and to "beggars".

I just don't understand "Happy are the poor in spirit". If you're happy then you're high in spirits, surely?

To examine this further, let's look at the word ptochoi. According to my Greek Lexicon[3], it means poor "in" something when combined with a genitive noun, however the word for spirit, pneumati, is dative and not genitive. For the meaning to be "poor in spirit", I would expect "to pneumato" rather than "to pneumati".

Looking at other uses of "to pneumati" in the bible, not including those where there is a preposition, which

---

[3] Liddell and Scott's Greek-English Lexicon (7th Edition 1889)

would add further clarity, these are some examples of many:

> John 11:33
> ἐνεβριμήσατο τῷ πνεύματι καὶ ἐτάραξεν
> He was deeply moved in spirit and was troubled…

> Acts 18:25
> ζέων τῷ πνεύματι ἐλάλει καὶ
> and being fervent in spirit, he was speaking…

> 1 Corinthians 14:15
> ψαλῶ τῷ πνεύματι ψαλῶ δὲ
> I will sing with the spirit and I will sing…

I get a sense of strength of emotion when using "in spirit", a bit like when we use the term "spirited", particularly this last example in Corinthians, I think "spirited", as an adjective, could be what is meant here.

The interpretation I'd like to put forward is "Happy and spirited are beggars".

The second part of the sentence echoes Luke, though the words are slightly different. Whereas Luke says "for the kingdom of God is yours", Matthew says "for the kingdom of the heavens is theirs".

As before, I'd suggest that ownership of the kingdom of the heavens means ownership of those things that abound in the kingdom of the heavens: love, joy, harmony, ecstasy, beauty, peace. God's love is there equally for everyone, God's peace is something that we get from true acceptance and understanding of that love.

This echoes the "blessed" versus "happy" discussion – we are all blessed, just as we are all loved, but we don't all feel happy, and we don't all feel God's peace, unless we focus on those blessings and on God's love.

One more point about the kingdom of the heavens – it is the opposite of the kingdom of earth. The kingdom of earth contains all things that are human or "of the world". The kingdom of earth is ruled by man and obeys certain laws. I'm not talking about the laws or constitutions of each nation, I'm talking about the laws of nature. What you get in the kingdom of earth is those things that are, largely, explainable in science. In the kingdom of the heavens you get the non-physical, the spiritual realm, and you get the source of miracles.

Think of the sense of awe and wonder that comes from witnessing a miracle. That's the kind of spirit-soaring joy that the disciples have.

Jesus is looking at the disciples when he speaks, therefore I'd suggest we can refer to those who are happy as "these men":

> *These men are happy and spirited, despite being beggars, because they have God's peace.*

Those who Mourn

Luke 6:21 (first part)

Μακάριοι οἱ κλαίοντες νῦν, Ὅτι γελάσετε.

Makarioi hoi klaiontes nyn, hoti gelasete.

Happy (are) the weeping now, for you will laugh.

When we go back to Luke, we switch from the subject being "they" (disciples) to "you" (disciples).

We have klaiontes, which means to weep, to lament, to mourn. It's a present participle, which means it behaves like a noun, ie "the weeping", or "the ones weeping", or, as it's commonly translated "those who mourn".

Since it behaves like a noun, the form gives us a clue as to who is mourning or grieving. It's nominative, masculine, plural, just like makarioi, therefore applies to the disciples.

The use of present tense, "mourning", is emphasised by the word for "now", as opposed to the use of the future tense for "you will laugh".

When will you laugh? What will make you laugh? We don't get any clues.

This calls to mind someone I know whose husband died, who said to me "I feel I shall never be truly happy again". Her world had changed beyond recognition and her grief was all-consuming.

Laughter is a visible display of happiness, just as weeping is to sorrow. Both come as a reaction to something. Something nice or happy might make you smile, but laughter requires something else as well. It's often triggered by a surprise – a joke with a punchline that's unexpected, a bit of slapstick, something ridiculous. You have to be in the right state of mind, and be sufficiently relaxed, to be able to laugh.

Saying "you will laugh" suggests that you'll be able to put aside your troubles, be entertained and enjoy life.

When you know that there is hope, in fact promise, of care-free laughter in the future, today's woes become bearable. You just have to trust.

> *You are happy, despite being upset now, because you will laugh again.*

Happiness Point 2: Trust

There are many things that we're told will happen to the disciples in the future, this being the first. We can get hung up on questions such as when, or how, this could possibly happen, but maybe the point is that they, and we, should simply trust in God. If we can do that, happiness now can be ours.

If I could keep my focus on what is in front of me and leave the future to God, how much simpler and easier life would be. If I had sufficient faith to say that whatever happens, if I trust in God, I will find a way forward and I will find happiness, I'd never be afraid again. I'd endure any kind of hardship and any kind of pain. I might not necessarily always get the outcome exactly in the way I might expect, but I'll get the right outcome for me. How liberating would that be?

And yet I struggle with trust sometimes. I find myself obsessing about something, from time to time, or trying to problem-solve a problem that isn't mine to solve. When I know I can trust God, why do I find it hard to let go and let God look after things for me?

I had an incident recently that showed me something about my feelings of trust.

I had tickets to see my favourite band. They were expensive tickets, a major band in a small venue a few hours away, and I felt very lucky to have managed to get them. I couldn't wait.

On the day of the concert, though, one of my teenage daughters became ill. What should I do? I convinced myself she didn't seem too bad and we decided to still go. When I was sitting in my seat, waiting for the performance to start, I checked my phone and saw a message suggesting she was getting worse not better, and her sister was obviously quite worried. I replied with some advice as to what to do and tried to focus on enjoying the concert. I offered up a prayer that she be kept safe.

Inevitably it took the shine off the evening. We decided to leave early, to get a swift exit, avoiding the crowds, and to get the earlier train. But when we got to the station, we found that all trains for the rest of the night were cancelled. It looked like we were stuck and wouldn't be able to get back till the morning.

Now lots of emotions were coming up inside me, including a sense of panic. I obviously shouldn't have gone, I'd been selfish. How could I expect to enjoy myself when I was neglecting my role as a mother? The cancelled trains seemed like a punishment from God – what had I been thinking?

Was this the explanation? My daughter's health was at risk because I hadn't done what I should do.

Or was there another explanation?

I'd prayed "Please God, keep her from getting worse", but I hadn't let go. I'd carried on obsessing "she should be ok because…", "I'm sure she'll be alright because…", "if the worst happens they can always…" I was praying but I wasn't trusting at all.

I wasn't trusting my prayer would be answered because I didn't believe my prayer *should* be answered, because I believed more in my own guilt than in anything else.

I didn't deserve an answered prayer because I'd done wrong. It wasn't right that I should enjoy myself and have a smooth journey back because I had to fully learn my lesson. I had to appreciate the error of my ways and take my punishment.

Then I had a moment of clarity. I saw the lack of trust for what it was. I'd prayed but I hadn't let go, because I hadn't felt worthy of the answer to the prayer. I began to see that my feelings of unworthiness and guilt weren't serving anyone at all.

I prayed a new prayer: "I trust my journey home to you." Then I truly relaxed and surrendered the way forward to God, feeling no anxiety.

We found we could go to another station and get a train that didn't take us home, but took us close enough to get a lift from a friend. We got home, hardly any later than originally planned, to find the poorly daughter asleep and the other relieved to see us and now able to sleep herself.

As a result of this I've realised that I need to ask myself, when I'm praying for something, whether I trust that God will deliver it. If I don't believe I'm worthy of answered prayer then it's like driving with the brakes on. I need to learn to take my foot of the brake pedal and let God take me forward as only He can.

Do I believe in a God that punishes? No, I don't.

Do I believe I punish myself? Yes, all the time. This is what needs to stop.

Matthew 5:4

μακάριοι οἱ πενθοῦντες, ὅτι αὐτοὶ παρακληθήσονται.

makarioi hoi penthountes, hoti autoi paraklethesontai.

Happy (are) the grieving, for they will be comforted.

Penthountes comes from the verb pentheo, which means "I grieve" or "I mourn".

Why are they happy? For (hoti) they/themselves (autoi) will be comforted (paraklethesontai)

The verb is in the passive voice, which means an action will be done *to* the subject of the sentence, not done *by* the subject of the sentence. It's a future tense, they will be comforted in the future. It's third person plural, so we can be sure it goes with "they", the ones who are happy and the ones who are grieving.

Ok, so they can be happy because they know they won't always be sad, because they will be comforted.

These first Beatitudes are all about opposites. The opposites here are grief. mourning or loss, on the one hand, and comfort on the other.

When will they be comforted? We don't know.

Who will they be comforted by? Jesus doesn't say. The context, from the previous verse, could suggest that since they have God's peace, this is what will provide them comfort.

The word autoi could simply be giving emphasis to who we're talking about, "they", as in "they will be comforted", the inference being "unlike those of you that don't know God's peace".

Or it could mean "themselves". The word "autoi", or "autos", forms part of "automatic" and "automobile etc, and means "by itself". Could it mean "they will be comforted by themselves"?

The evidence for this isn't perhaps compelling based on grammar alone, but I think the context could support this interpretation. If you know God's peace, you don't need anyone or anything, you can be happy, and you know how to find comfort, by yourself.

Happiness Point 3: You don't need anything else

When we grieve, or mourn the loss of someone, there tends to be more than one emotion at play.

A friend of mine died a few years ago. She'd been ill for a long time so in a way I was expecting it, yet the phone call still came as a shock. Death seems so final – where there's life there's hope, but death says that the battle has been lost, the game's over.

For me, after the initial shock came regret. I wish I'd done more. I wish I'd said things to her that perhaps I'd felt too awkward to say. Now the chance was gone and the opportunity missed.

There was also anger. I don't know why she had to get ill and why she couldn't be cured. It wasn't fair.

Then came the sense of loss. I missed her more initially, but I still miss her now.

Comfort for me came in a few ways. A friend suggested that I find a quiet moment and say out loud everything I wished I'd said to her, just as if she was sitting in the room with me. This proved to be extremely cathartic. It helped me to structure my thoughts, to unravel what it was that I really felt. I've used this since, with relatives that have died, and each time it's enabled me to find a sense of closure that might otherwise have eluded me. Call me crazy, but I actually think the spirit of the deceased can hear these communications. Each time I've used this approach it has made me feel so much better.

Anger can be hard to get over when someone dies before you feel their time is right, when they still have so much to contribute and, as in her case, when they have dependent children. It did dissipate, for me, when I accepted that I don't understand why, and should never expect to understand why, some things happen.

As life moved on for me and I got used to her not being there, the pain of loss reduced. My life without her grew so that the part she occupied became relatively reduced. Maybe I grew closer to one or two other friends in the process of losing her.

I guess you could say I found peace in relation to the loss of my friend. Peace instead of regret, peace instead of anger, and peace instead of loneliness. It took me a while, and it involved me understanding myself a little more than I had previously, but I managed to find my way back to peace.

Peace had been my aim, without realising it. I knew that I needed to make peace with my feelings of regret and my sense of anger and frustration.

The simple fact of knowing that peace is possible means it becomes more achievable.

I think that when Jesus refers to the disciples and says that they will find comfort when they mourn, he's saying their ability to find peace is more attuned, such that they don't need to be concerned in the face of grief and mourning.

God's peace is there, it's never going away. Our connection with it varies according to what's going on with us, but it's always available if we know how to reach it.

We have to, ourselves, find our way to all that is available to us, and the way to do that is to better understand ourselves. What took us away from God's peace in the first place?

To know ourselves is to know what stops us from being able to feel God's peace. What we need is to know why we react the way we do, or why we beat ourselves up for something we've done or not done, in relation to someone we've lost.

In my case I felt guilt for not being a more attentive friend, and guilt for not expressing myself more clearly with her. I wanted to be able to help her get better and I couldn't. Nothing I could have done might have made any difference to her and the timing of her death, but understanding my feelings made a difference to me and my acceptance of her passing.

I realised the guilt did me no good, it simply brought me down and tainted my memories of her. It's only when I let go of feelings of guilt that I was able to think about her with nothing but love.

I think many of us have this tendency to feelings of unreasonable guilt. The answer doesn't come from outside of us, it comes from developing a new level of honesty and understanding of ourselves.

We have within us everything we need in every situation. We have access to God's peace. If we're not feeling God's peace, it's up to us to ask ourselves why we can't connect with it. We just have to work out why it is that we're pulling ourselves in the wrong direction. The onus is on us.

We can ask for strength to carry us through difficult situations, but really we already have access to that strength, we just may not be using it. It's like asking the sun to shine more brightly when actually we're sitting inside a cave.

The route to happiness is to ask myself why I spend so much time avoiding God's peace.

In talking about sadness followed by comfort, could it be that Jesus is saying it is better to be happy after having been sad? If you have known sadness, you can then appreciate what it is to overcome it. You can appreciate the good times because you've been through the bad. Also it's often the way that sadness teaches us something about ourselves, and if we can understand it then we're better for the experience.

If you'd never known any sadness then you wouldn't know how to deal with it, or that it is possible to overcome it, and you wouldn't necessarily know how to find comfort.

Happiness Point 4: You can learn from your hardship

Nobody enjoys difficult times. We don't understand why things had to be this way – what did I do to deserve this?

I don't think we can expect to understand why bad things happen. All we can do is face what we have in front of us, without knowing why it is in front of us. There will be some form of lesson available to us, if we're willing and able to see it and take it on.

Sometimes we can see how we ended up here, sometimes we understand how the choices we made led us to a point where it all went sour. Perhaps we have to go the wrong way, to experience what we don't want, before we work out the right way, and get clarity on what we do want.

Sometimes we don't know how we ended up here. Some people seem to be born to hardship, of any and all kinds, often those who seem to deserve it the least. Alternatively there are others who seem to live a charmed life from the outset.

Worse than our own hardships, it's hard to watch our loved ones go through difficult times. Sometimes, though, that's exactly what we have to do. Watch them go through something painful as we stand helpless on the side-lines, or watch them do something we know will end in tears and just be ready for when the tears come.

I do believe, though, that to have gone through hardship generally leaves us better equipped at dealing with hardship in the future. I coped with it before, so I can cope with it again. Or, if I can cope with this, I can cope with anything.

These men are happy, even when they are grieving, because they know that they will find comfort.

The Meek

There is no equivalent verse in Luke on the subject of the meek.

Matthew 5:5

> μακάριοι οἱ πραεῖς, ὅτι αὐτοὶ κληρονομήσουσιν τὴν γῆν.

> makarioi hoi praeis, hoti autoi kleronomesousin ten gen.

> Happy (are) the meek, for they will inherit the earth.

The word praeis means mild or gentle. Unlike beggars and those who mourn, it's not immediately obvious where this could be going – why shouldn't they be happy?

They are happy for they, or they themselves (autoi), will inherit (kleronomesousin) the earth (ten gen). Ownership of the earth will fall to them, at some point in the future.

What about the warriors, the fighters, the aggressors and invaders? What about those who work hard at influencing those around them, making themselves known, canvassing good opinion, in order to put themselves in prime position for an inheritance? No, it's the mild and gentle way that wins out in the end. The ones that push for it the least will end up taking the lot.

Here we have a great irony – those who don't strive to own land will end up being the ones the land belongs to.

In what way will they inherit the earth? Will they inherit in the way that we might inherit a family member's house and then sell it for financial gain? Or does it mean ownership in the sense of control? Will they be the ones with responsibility for the stewardship of this world that we live in? Will they be the ones in charge, making the decisions?

When will they inherit the earth? Tomorrow, next year, at the end of time, or in death?

To inherit the earth on death doesn't make sense, surely, since that's the point when the earth is of no use to you. This must mean either at some point during the disciples' lives, or it's a more generic point, referring to the end of time.

Given that the disciples lived 2000 years ago, perhaps we might we have expected the meek to have inherited the earth by now? I'm not sure we could say they have. I wouldn't describe our world leaders as meek, nor our biggest land owners.

What is this saying then?

One thing is for sure, Jesus is advocating the way of the meek, or gentle and mild. To inherit the earth sounds like a good thing, success, you might say, and the way to be successful in this way is to be mild and gentle. It could be interpreted that Jesus is saying the secret of success is not to try too hard.

The word inherit is quite passive – it's like saying "good things will come to you". Perhaps that's the point. Be gentle and mild and good things will come to you, you don't have to chase for everything. Then of course you can be happy now, secure in the knowledge that good things will come, without you even having to try.

Happiness Point 5: Don't try too hard

We all tend to get caught up in some form of hamster wheel, where we struggle on, trying our best, trying to force people to do the things we want them to do, getting upset when they don't. I don't believe this is the way to happiness.

Peace doesn't have to try.

Sometimes in our desire to achieve a particular outcome we lose a sense of perspective and we feel we have to keep battling on, no matter how hard we have to work. I don't think this needs to be the way.

I'm not suggesting we shouldn't try at all, just that I don't think we get marks for effort alone, when there might be a better way of achieving what we want.

What if we were to establish an intention, then let God help it to happen, peacefully, without fuss. God can show us to the win-win situations, letting objections fall away without argument and rancour.

Let go and let God, you might say.

When I used to work in project management, I spent a lot of time chasing people. Often, getting results required terrier-like tenacity.

I remember one occasion when, as a matter of urgency, with very short notice, I needed to bring together two people, who were both notoriously difficult to get hold of, to get a decision made. They were both rarely in the office and their diaries tended to be booked up weeks in advance, so I didn't fancy my chances.

I'd taken to using prayer within my day job a lot more – just in my mind, between me and God. Whereas in the past I might have worked very hard to badger these people, or the people that managed their diaries, pushing hard for the earliest meeting they could manage. Instead, having offered up a prayer, I had a sudden urge to go to the canteen. There in the canteen I saw one of the people I needed to speak to, walking away from the till, and I spied the other, just about to join the queue to buy a coffee. Their paths were literally crossing right in front of me. I seized my moment, grabbed them both and explained the issue, and in a minute or two had the decision I'd been after.

This is one example of many I could give, where me doing less and God doing more has brought about a far better solution than if I'd tried, even with all my might, on my own.

When we hand things over to God we are trying less, being less aggressive, competitive or obsessive. And in trying less, we're achieving far more.

These men, whose way is gentle and mild, are happy, for they know good things will come to them.

The Hungry

Luke 6:21 (second part)

> Μακάριοι οἱ πεινῶντες νῦν, Ὅτι χορτασθήσεσθε.

> Makarioi hoi peinontes nyn, Hoti chortasthesesthe

> Happy (are) the hungry now, for you will be satisfied

Peinontes is from the word that means famished. It can also mean striving for something. This passage can either be taken literally – "don't worry about being hungry now, because you will have all the food you need", or figuratively – "it is good to strive, to desire earnestly, now, because you will get what you need".

We're talking about the future again. So far we've had those who mourn will be comforted, the meek will inherit the earth, and here we're saying those who are hungry will be satisfied (chortasthesesthe). The suggestion is that however bleak things are now, better days are to come.

One way of interpreting this is that Jesus is simply saying "don't worry". Good things will happen to the disciples, (Happiness Point 2 again), everything will work out fine, because they are disciples, because they know God, because they have God's peace.

Wanting food, or striving for something you desire, is not a bad thing. Life has its ups and downs. Perhaps we should enjoy being hungry because then food is all the more enjoyable. Perhaps the fact that your football team has lost or drawn so many games makes the 3-0 victory all the more sweet. Perhaps we should enjoy life's struggles, because when the struggle is over then we can enjoy no longer struggling. Perhaps we learn from the struggle, and the struggle makes us ultimately stronger and able to cope with further struggle in the future.

It is not "you will be satisfied" that makes you happy, it's the fact that you *know* you will be satisfied.

> *You are happy, even though you're hungry now, because you know you will be satisfied.*

Matthew 5:6

> μακάριοι οἱ πεινῶντες καὶ διψῶντες τὴν δικαιοσύνην, ὅτι αὐτοὶ χορτασθήσονται.

> makarioi hoi peinontes kai dipsontes ten dikaiosynen, hoti autoi chortasthesontai.

> Happy (are) the hungry and thirsty for justice, for they will be satisfied.

Matthew's version suggests we may have been right to think of Luke's words as being more figurative than literal. The disciples are hungry and thirsty for justice, or righteousness. They will be satisfied (chortasthesesthe), which is the same word that Luke uses.

Again Matthew uses the word for "they" or "themselves" (autoi).

This suggests that the disciples, and presumably anyone else who strives for justice, will get justice. There's an inference that they don't have justice now, since the justice they seek is not the sense of justice that abounds in popular opinion, which is why they strive for it, but this is a form of encouragement. Don't stop trying, the right way will come good.

> *These men are happy, who strive for justice, because they know justice will prevail.*

The Merciful

There is no equivalent verse in Luke on the subject of the merciful, as with the next few verses in Matthew.

Matthew 5:7

> μακάριοι οἱ ἐλεήμονες, ὅτι αὐτοὶ ἐλεηθήσονται.
>
> makarioi hoi eleemones, hoti autoi eleethesontai.
>
> Happy (are) the merciful, for they will receive mercy.

They are happy for they themselves (autoi) will receive mercy.

Eleemones comes from the word for having pity or showing mercy and compassion.

This is a promise to the disciples – just as they show mercy, so they will receive mercy. This brings to mind Matthew 7:12 "Do to others whatever you would like them to do to you".

There is a question of emphasis, I believe. Of all the many things Jesus could have suggested as the right way to behave, we have the importance of being mild and gentle, and now to be merciful, to show compassion. This is an important part of forgiveness. When you look at someone else, don't judge them or turn away from them, but think how it would be to be like them.

The tense is future, which suggests this may not be the case at this point in time, but in the future they will reap what they are sowing today.

Are we to infer the disciples weren't shown mercy and compassion at this point? Quite possibly this would have been true. They followed Jesus, and whilst that would be a source of envy for some, for others it would be cause for scorn and derision.

The message is clear – be happy in the certain knowledge that, just as you show mercy, so you will be shown mercy when you need it.

Happiness Point 6: Show mercy

Mercy and forgiveness are key when it comes to living peacefully. We won't always agree with everyone around us, we have to accept that sometimes we won't see eye to eye. We don't have to all behave the same just as we don't all think the same. Tolerance and a lack of judgement are what we need to show others, and when the tables are turned, we'll get tolerance and a lack of judgement in return.

If happiness is the aim, how can we think we'll achieve it if we carry around unforgiveness? Unforgiveness will always have the power to bring down our mood, whenever we remember the person or the thing that we can't forgive.

Forgiveness is acceptance of what has happened. Whether I condone it or not, whether I want it to have happened or not, it doesn't matter. I can't change the past. I have to accept it and move on.

Forgiveness isn't about who's right and who's wrong. Most people usually think they're right, or at least excusable, and they do what they do for reasons others may not be aware of.

Achieving forgiveness where we feel wronged is, I believe, the most significant and valuable lesson we'll ever learn. The question is not *whether* we should forgive someone, but *how* we can forgive someone, regardless of the extent to which we feel wronged. I refer to this in more detail in "My Lord's Prayer"[4].

The other side of showing mercy, one that I think can be overlooked, is that we must show mercy on ourselves. We give ourselves such a hard time, we expect so much from ourselves. Sometimes it feels like we have to be everything to everyone, all the time, and that's just not possible.

People pleasing is exhausting, and pleasing everyone is just not possible. We need to balance it by showing mercy and compassion to ourselves, let ourselves off the hook.

From the smallest transgression to the worst wrongdoing, the way to peace is always the same. As it says in the Lord's Prayer, I should forgive in the same way that God forgives – always, all the time.

These men who show mercy are happy, for they know they will receive mercy.

---

[4] My Lord's Prayer by Jean Webb, Spontaneous Life Publishing

The Pure in Heart

Matthew 5:8

> μακάριοι οἱ καθαροὶ τῇ καρδίᾳ, ὅτι αὐτοὶ τὸν Θεὸν ὄψονται.

> makarioi hoi katharoi te kardia, hoti autoi ton Theon opsontai.

> Happy (are) the clear in heart, for they will see God for themselves.

This is generally translated as "Blessed are the pure in heart". The word katharoi means clear or clean.

Following from the question of whether "Blessed are the poor in spirit" could be "Blessed in spirit are the poor", I have a similar question here. We have nominative plural "blessed" and "the pure", followed by dative singular "in heart". Could it be that we should read this as "Blessed in heart are the pure"?

We would know from the way the words were spoken, even with the same order, through the emphasis given. It would either be "Blessed are the pure-in-heart" or "Blessed are the pure, in heart."

There is no example I can find of katharoi, pure, being followed by "in". The same word occurs 3 times in John (13:10, 13:11 and 15:3), all generally translated to be "clean". There are references to "pure heart", where both pure and heart have the same form (1 Timothy 1:5 and 2:22, 1 Peter 1:22).

The words "te kardia" are used in many other places, for example Matthew 11:29, which the New Living Translation has as "I am humble and gentle at heart".

There could, however, be a clue in the use of what follows "for they will see God". There is generally a link between the first and second half of these statements. Clarity is linked to vision. Therefore if you have clarity, or purity, of mind or vision, you see clearly, and you see God.

Technically, opsontai is in the middle voice, which means it should be translated as "they will see God for themselves. When this is combined with Matthew's use of autoi for they/themselves, I wonder if we should read into this that the disciples are equipped with everything they need, themselves (Happiness Point 3).

What does it mean to see God? To feel God's peace and to witness God's miracles. These men are not focused on the world around them, not taken in by things that might seem to others to be a source of happiness, they know where true happiness lies.

They need to be clear, or pure, of things that would affect their ability to see God. They need to keep their windows clean, figuratively. Or if we think of a pond, it can either be settled and clear, or it can be muddied by being stirred up. What things muddy the water? Those things that are best left as they are. Those things we don't need to focus on, things that distract us unnecessarily, things that don't contribute to our higher purpose. I'd suggest this could cover all manner of concerns and anxieties that we could let go of.

We need to have the ability to be still, focused and allow clarity to come through.

Happiness Point 7: Clarity

If I want to see God but my mind is cluttered with an endless stream of thoughts, then answers to my prayers might not get through. By quietening the voice that gets caught up on the same thought processes, over and over, I stand a better chance of achieving clarity.

I struggle with this. I problem-solve imaginary situations, or I play back in my mind something I've done or said (was I right to do or say that?). I get so lost in my thoughts that I don't see things that are right in front of me.

I know that inspiration, or creative ideas, are more likely to strike me when I'm not chasing them, and when I've brought my attention back to the moment.

I need to try less and to think less, and allow more of God to come through.

The way I would interpret this verse is:

> *These men with clarity are happy, for they know they will see God for themselves.*

The Peacemakers

Matthew 5:9

> μακάριοι οἱ εἰρηνοποιοί, ὅτι αὐτοὶ υἱοὶ Θεοῦ κληθήσονται.

> makarioi hoi eirenopoioi, hoti autoi huioi Theou klethesontai.

> Happy (are) the peacemakers, for they will the sons of God be called.

Eirene means peace (like the name Irene), poioi means makers, so we are saying "Happy are the peacemakers". They (autoi) will be called (klethesontai) the sons (huioi) of God (Theou).

There are no opposites here. Why should peacemakers be the sons of God? What does Jesus mean when he talks of sons of God?

There are echoes of the reference to the meek. Being warrior-like, aggressive and competitive might make you feel that you're accomplishing something, but true accomplishment – inheriting the earth or, in this case, being called a son of God – is for the mild, the gentle and the peacemakers.

God is father to us all, which would make us all sons and daughters, but I think what's referred to here was more than that. Jesus was alive in the time of the Roman Empire, and Roman emperors used to choose trusted generals as successors, rather than succession passing to their actual offspring. They would adopt sons in order to pass the empire on to their candidate of choice.

This level of honour is I think what is referred to here. There is a sense of being chosen and being trusted. They achieve this honour not by being competitive and trying to outdo the competition, they get it by striving for peace.

> *These men who strive for peace are happy, for they will be chosen by God*

The Persecuted

There are similar accounts in Matthew and Luke on this subject.

Matthew 5:10

> μακάριοι οἱ δεδιωγμένοι ἕνεκεν δικαιοσύνης, ὅτι αὐτῶν ἐστιν ἡ βασιλεία τῶν οὐρανῶν.

> makarioi hoi dediogmenoi heneken dikaiosynes, hoti auton estin he basileia ton ouranon.

> Happy (are) those who have been pursued on account of justice, for theirs is the kingdom of the heavens.

Dediogmenoi is from the word dioko that means to pursue, chase or hunt, hence the common translation, in every bible version I've seen, being "persecuted".

Dikaiosynes means righteousness or justice. Why should you be persecuted on account of justice? Why would anyone pursue you for being righteous? Whose justice and whose righteousness are we talking about?

The answer lies in who is doing the pursing. They must think *they* are the righteous and just ones, they think that the disciples are lacking in righteousness and justice.

Why would you chase or hunt someone for what they believe in? What are you going to do when you catch them? If I didn't agree with someone I wouldn't chase them. I'd do the opposite, I'd avoid them.

An alternative translation of dioko is to drive away. This summons up an image of angry people waving their fists and booing, saying "you're not welcome here with your ridiculous ideas, go away!"

This is the cancel culture of the time. It's not enough that I don't agree with you, I have to stop you from spreading lies to anyone else. I have to run you out of town.

Whether we use "persecuted" or "driven away", the sense is the same. We don't want you expressing your opinions here. I like the word "hounded". Dogs, when on the attack, can either chase you, or if you don't run, they have other ways of silencing you.

This continues the theme of being mild/gentle, a peacemaker, as opposed to an aggressor, the pursuer or hunter. Let them judge you to be wrong, let them hunt you down for what you believe in, for the kingdom of heaven is there for you.

This is about not minding what other people think of you. Closeness to God matters more than anything else.

Happiness Point 8: Don't worry about what others think

How refreshing would it be to never care what other people think of me? How much worry would be lifted from me?

In fact, I find it very hard to imagine, as the vast majority of my negative thoughts are either playing over in my mind something that I've said or done ("will they think I was wrong?"), or imagining future conversations when I don't think I'm in full agreement with someone ("how will I tell them I don't agree?").

Maybe it's just me, maybe everyone else is sufficiently self-confident not to be overly concerned with how they're seen by others. I doubt it somehow.

Concern for the way others see us is what leads to a lack of transparency ("I can't say I didn't like that cake/painting/dress/hairstyle"), to doing things we don't want to do ("I don't want to do this but I can't say no"), to, in some cases, sleepless nights over imagined differences.

Or is it just me?

Why do I care so much? I don't know. I see the same thing in people round me all the time – doing things for appearances sake, not wanting to upset the apple cart, making life complicated by wanting to avoid a conflict or an uncomfortable situation.

If we didn't care what people thought of us we'd have fewer situation comedies, that's for sure. The plot of 30-minute comedies often centres around somebody not wanting to own up to a truth, and going to great lengths to cover their tracks.

If we didn't care what people thought of us we'd never be in the situation where we say one thing to one person and something different to another. We wouldn't talk about people behind their backs, we'd say what we have to say to their face. What a simpler world that would be.

I need to be true to myself. If someone likes me because I do what they want, or say what they want to hear, and I'm not being true to myself, their good opinion is worth nothing, and I lose my own sense of authenticity. If I'm true to myself and I lose friends as a result, perhaps they weren't true friends.

All that matters is that I do my best to do right by God. If anyone doesn't like it then that's just tough. I won't get it right always, but I can get back on track when I go in the wrong direction. I just have to have confidence that as I forgive others, I'll be forgiven when I make mistakes.

The fact that this is aimed at the disciples is particularly important, because it is their definition of righteousness and justice that is to be defended, not the view accepted by those who would disagree with them.

> *These men are happy, despite being hounded for their beliefs, for they have God's peace.*

When They Insult You

Matthew 5:11

> μακάριοί ἐστε ὅταν ὀνειδίσωσιν ὑμᾶς καὶ διώξωσιν καὶ εἴπωσιν πᾶν πονηρὸν καθ' ὑμῶν ψευδόμενοι ἕνεκεν ἐμοῦ.

> makarioi este hotan oneidisosin hymas kai dioxosin kai eiposin pan poneron kath' hymon pseudomenoi heneken emou.

> Happy are you when they shall insult you and pursue (you) and shall say all bad things about you lying on account of me.

We get a verb for the first time, in relation to being blessed. "Este" means "you are". This is a change from earlier verses where Matthew is referring to the disciples in the third person, "they". Is this significant? Are we to think that Matthew is still talking to the crowd about the disciples, only this time facing them and addressing them as "you", or has he turned his gaze to the crowd and is now addressing them?

There's a mix of tenses: blessed are you (este, present tense) when they shall insult you (oneidisosin, future tense). You are happy now, and you will continue being happy when men shall insult you. They will pursue you, (dioxosin, future tense – the same verb as dediogmenoi in the previous verse), and say (poneron, future tense) all bad things (pan poneron) about you (kath'hymon).

The last part of the verse explains the behaviour further: lying (pseudomenoi, present tense) on account of me (heneken emou).

But, hang on a minute – what does "on account of" (heneken) refer to? Does it mean, as it is commonly translated, "telling lies about you on account of me", or could it mean "you are happy… on account of me", or "you are happy… because of your association with me"? That makes more sense to me.

Regardless, the subjects of the sentence are being prepared for a rough ride. They're going to be insulted, castigated, ridiculed, lied about, but it won't dent their happiness.

Of this list, to be lied about would irk me the most. People can disagree with me, fair enough, but to have someone deliberately tell lies about me, slander me, would cause me to feel very frustrated. People go to great lengths to clear their name when they feel they've been misreprented.

The disciples were prepared to face all of this, not to challenge it or fight it, but to accept it, uncomplaining, and their happiness was unaffected by the prospect.

> *You are happy, despite the fact you will be insulted and hounded and bad things will be said about you, telling lies, because of your connection with me.*

Matthew 5:12

> χαίρετε καὶ ἀγαλλιᾶσθε, ὅτι ὁ μισθὸς ὑμῶν πολὺς ἐν τοῖς οὐρανοῖς· οὕτως γὰρ ἐδίωξαν τοὺς προφήτας τοὺς πρὸ ὑμῶν.

> chairete kai agalliasthe, hoti ho misthos hymon polys en tois ouranois; houtos gar edioxan tous prophetas tous pro hymon.

> Rejoice and be joyful, for the payment of you (is) great in the heavens. For in this way they pursued the prophets before you.

Don't just be happy – jump for joy and be delighted! Chairete means "rejoice" and galliasthe means "rejoice exceedingly". Both are second person plural, a command to the subjects, be it the disciples or the wider group.

The payment (misthos) is many or great (polys), in the heavens (en tois ouranois). Again we're differentiating between what happens on earth and what happens in heaven. The temptation is to assume this means "when you die", but I think of it generally as a spiritual reward, the reference to the heavens underlining the distinction from any form of earthly payment.

In this way (houtos), they pursued or hounded (edioxan, past tense, same verb as dioxosin and dediogmenoi) the prophets before you (tous prohetas tous pro hymon).

This is referencing those from previous generations who knew the truth – they also were insulted and ridiculed. That didn't stop them and that didn't stop their words from being recorded and passed on from generation to generation. Being rejected by society at large is not a problem, when you are guided by God, and, thinking of the prophets, you're in good company.

> *Be glad, be delighted! For your spirit will be rewarded. The prophets of the past were treated this way too.*

The account in Luke is very similar:

Luke 6:22

> Μακάριοί ἐστε ὅταν μισήσωσιν ὑμᾶς οἱ ἄνθρωποι, καὶ ὅταν ἀφορίσωσιν ὑμᾶς καὶ ὀνειδίσωσιν καὶ ἐκβάλωσιν τὸ ὄνομα ὑμῶν ὡς πονηρὸν ἕνεκα τοῦ Υἱοῦ τοῦ ἀνθρώπου.

> makarioi este hotan misesosin hymas hoi anthropoi, kai hotan aphorisosin hymas kai oneidisosin kai ekbalosin to onoma hymon hos poneron heneka tou Huiou tou anthropou.

> Happy are you when men shall hate you, and when they shall exclude you and shall insult (you), and shall cast out the name of you as evil on account of the son of man.

Again we get a verb for the first time, in relation to being blessed. "Este" means "you are", which is a continuation of the use of the second person, ie "blessed" is in relation to "you", the disciples.

As in Matthew, there's a mix of tenses: blessed are you now (present tense) when men shall hate you (misesosin, future tense). They will exclude you, (aphirsosin, future tense), and insult you, (oneidisosin, future tense), and throw out, (ekbalosin, future tense), your name (to onoma hymon) as evil (hos poneron). The use of name could have the sense of reputation, your reputation will be ruined.

The reason for all this? On account of the Son of man (heneka tou Huiou tou anthropou). I have the same question I had in Matthew's account – does it mean "they shall cast out your name as evil on account of the son of man", or does it mean "You are happy... on account of the son of man". I don't think it changes the sense of the passage in any way, I just find it interesting that it's commonly translated one way, when to me it works slightly better when viewed the other way.

The point is that the thing that causes you to be happy is the same as the thing that causes you to be rubbished as you will be.

Son (Huiou) has a capital and refers to Jesus. Jesus refers to himself as the son of man, rather than son of God. This suggests to me that he did not see himself as superior to those around him. He came as a link between us and God, for our sake, as our servant, as our son.

At this point the disciples might not have been hated, excluded and insulted. Perhaps this is the reason for the pep talk. In addition to what you've experienced up to now, being poor, hungry and sad, you're also going to be hated, excluded and insulted.

But you won't care.

> *You are happy, despite the fact you will be hated, excluded and insulted, your reputation in ruins, because of your connection with me.*

Luke 6:23

> χάρητε ἐν ἐκείνῃ τῇ ἡμέρᾳ καὶ σκιρτήσατε· ἰδοὺ γὰρ ὁ μισθὸς ὑμῶν πολὺς ἐν τῷ οὐρανῷ· κατὰ τὰ αὐτὰ γὰρ ἐποίουν τοῖς προφήταις οἱ πατέρες αὐτῶν.

> charete en ekeine te hemera kai skirtesate; idou gar ho misthos hymon polys en to ourano; kata

ta auta gar epoioun tois prophetais hoi pateres auton.

Rejoice in that day and leap for joy. Behold for the payment for you is great in heaven. In the same way the prophets were treated by the fathers.

The word for rejoice (charete) is the same root as the word in Matthew, only in this instance it is a more immediate command, as is "leap for joy" (skiresate).

Behold (idou) is second person singular, which is strange, since Jesus is addressing more than one person. I take it to be like a casual "you see" that doesn't need to be taken literally, it is just to add a little emphasis.

As in Matthew, the promise is that there is a great payment for you in heaven (Luke uses the plural, "heavens").

The next part is best read back to front: likewise (auton) the fathers (hoi pateres) used to treat the prophets (epoioun tois prophetais) the same way (kata ta auta).

The fathers must mean the fathers of the people who are treating you badly – the sense being that the same treatment was given to the prophets in the past, by the descendants of those treating you this way.

But you won't care.

Be glad, dance for joy! Know that your spirit will be rewarded. Past generations also treated the prophets this way.

Woe to You

In Luke, Jesus goes on to explain clearly what he means with the use of opposites.

What is interesting here is that it's hard to believe he's still addressing the disciples. I think that either he turned his gaze from the disciples to the crowd for the last two verses, as he may have done in the corresponding verses in Matthew, as referenced by the change from they to you, or if not then he turns his gaze from the disciples to the crowd at this point.

Luke 6:24

> Πλὴν οὐαὶ ὑμῖν τοῖς πλουσίοις, Ὅτι ἀπέχετε τὴν παράκλησιν ὑμῶν.

> Plen ouai hymin tois plousiois, hoti apechete ten paraklesin hymon.

> But woe to you who are rich, for you are receiving the comfort of you.

The word ouai is an exclamation, in a way that you might say "Oh dear". You can imagine it being accompanied by a shake of the head. When translated as "woe to you" it feels to me like a prediction "woe will come to you", almost like a curse. I don't think this was what was intended. I could even put forward a case for it being a little bit of humour.

If you're rich (tois plousiois) and receiving comfort (apechete ten paraklesin) then the implication is that you aren't striving, that you're likely to be self-satisfied. If this is the case, and you think you have life cracked, you might not be in pursuit of true happiness, you might not feel any need for spiritual advancement.

I don't think this is a warning against the perils of being rich, rather I think the focus is on the comfort that you might get from being rich. Comfort from riches is not true happiness.

We can all think of people who've made it in terms of financial success, only for them to realise that this doesn't bring happiness. They get to a point where they have everything they ever wanted in terms of material things, only to realise they're not actually happy, and maybe there could be more to life.

Taking comfort in riches is not happiness.

Luke 6:25 (first part)

> Οὐαὶ ὑμῖν, οἱ ἐμπεπλησμένοι νῦν, Ὅτι πεινάσετε.
>
> Ouai hymin, hoi empeplesmenoi nyn, hoti peinasete.
>
> Woe to you, having been satisfied now, for you will be hungry.

If you're satisfied (empeplesmenoi) with what you have now, you will be hungry in the future (peinasete, future tense). The word for hungry is the same word used in verse 21.

What the world can give you is temporary. If your happiness depends on being full of food, or anything else that is of the world, when you don't get food, or whatever, from the world, you'll feel hungry.

Whereas if you're like the disciples and you can be happy regardless of whether you're full or hungry, you'll never worry about feeling hungry.

> *If your happiness is satisfied by things of the world, you will find that it won't last.*

Luke 6:25 (second part)

> Οὐαί, οἱ γελῶντες νῦν, Ὅτι πενθήσετε καὶ κλαύσετε.
>
> Ouai, hoi gelontes nyn, Hoti penthesete kai klausete.
>
> Woe to those who laugh now, for you will mourn and weep.

This is the opposite of Luke 6:21. The word for laugh (gelontes) is the same, as is weep (klausete). Therefore all the same points apply in reverse.

Jesus must be talking about those who are laughing, or who think they are happy, whose happiness doesn't come from knowing the truth about God. Their happiness can only be temporary, and they'll have no resilience, nothing to be a source of comfort, when things happen that cause them to mourn and weep.

Those who've never had to overcome difficulties won't know that they can overcome difficulties, and therefore won't be well equipped to do so in the future. Being satisfied now, with what you have, if you don't know God, will do you no good in the long run.

If you're happy with things as they are, without knowing God, you will be upset in the future.

Luke 6:26

Οὐαὶ ὅταν καλῶς ὑμᾶς εἴπωσιν πάντες οἱ ἄνθρωποι· Κατὰ τὰ αὐτὰ γὰρ ἐποίουν τοῖς ψευδοπροφήταις οἱ πατέρες αὐτῶν.

Ouai hotan kalos hymas eiposin pantes hoi anthropoi; kata ta auta gar epoioun tois pseudoprophetais hoi pateres auton.

Woe to you when all men speak well of you. In the same way were the false prophets treated by the fathers.

The order of the words means you have to go backwards and forwards to extract meaning: Oh dear (Ouai) when (hotan) all men (pantes hoi anthropoi) speak (eiposin) well (kalos) of you (hymas). The fathers (hoi pateres) used to treat (epoioun) the false prophets (tois pseudoprophetais) the same way (kata ta auta).

If men speak well of you, you shouldn't be happy, because previous generations used to speak well of the false prophets. The men that are referred to are "all men", (pantes hoi anthropoid), which is like saying "hoi polloi", which means "the masses", "the common people"[5].

---

[5] https://www.dictionary.com/browse/hoi-polloi

It doesn't matter if everyone disagrees with you, if everyone hates what you say, if everyone ridicules you, if you're with me and you're speaking God's truth, that is all that matters. Pandering to the crowd is not the answer.

> *Don't worry about what people think of you, because people traditionally think well of false prophets.*

My Beatitudes

Bringing together the interpretation from each verse, electing to go for the third person throughout, and merging verses from Matthew and Luke, this is what we get:

These men are happy and spirited, despite being beggars, because they have God's peace.

These men are happy, even when they are grieving, because they know that they will find comfort.

These men, whose way is gentle and mild, are happy, for they know good things will come to them.

These men are happy, who strive for justice, because they know justice will prevail.

These men who show mercy are happy, for they know they will receive mercy.

These men with clarity are happy, for they know they will see God for themselves.

These men who strive for peace are happy, for they will be chosen by God

These men are happy, despite being hounded for their beliefs, for they have God's peace.

These men are happy, despite the fact they will be hated, excluded and insulted, with reputations in ruins, because of their connection with me.

They can be glad and dance for joy. They know that their spirit will be rewarded. Past generations also treated the prophets this way.

Taking comfort in riches is not happiness.

Anyone whose happiness is satisfied by things of the world, will find that it won't last.

Anyone who is happy with things as they are, without knowing God, will be upset in the future.

No-one should worry about what other people think, because people traditionally think well of false prophets.

Happiness Points

Taking the points picked up from the analysis of the text, we have the following formula for happiness:

1. God's peace, not the things of the world, is what brings happiness
2. Trust that with God's peace, good things will come
3. You don't need anything else
4. You can learn from your hardship
5. Don't try too hard (be gentle and mild)
6. Show mercy
7. Allow clarity to come to you
8. Don't worry what others think.

Whenever I'm feeling challenged, disappointed, or in any way dissatisfied, I have to work my way through this list and ask myself where I am adrift from these points.

I would suggest this would require a good deal of re-programming and un-learning for the majority of people.

What doesn't help

There are some unhelpful myths that abound, with regard to improving happiness. These can be considered in the light of what the Beatitudes tells us.

1. Count your blessings

Naively, I actually thought this might form part of my summary for this analysis when I started. It didn't take long to realise that what most people would call blessings aren't necessarily the answer.

If someone suggested I count my blessings, I'd rattle off a list that includes my family, my house, my job, and so on. However, if you pick out from the Beatitudes what Jesus says about who is blessed and why, the reason they are blessed is not because they have any of these things. These things are more likely to be found in the "Woe to you" list in Luke. If I feel satisfied with this list of things and I don't "own God's kingdom" then I'm not blessed at all.

These things are, to a greater or lesser degree, transient. If my happiness depends on them then "Ouai" (oh dear!).

There is only one blessing that's worth counting – closeness to God, understanding how to find God, knowing what it is to feel God's peace.

2. There's always someone worse off

Likewise, I could look at someone who has no family, no house, no job, and so on, and I might think them worthy of pity, though it might be that they are blissfully happy, because they might be like the disciples. They might have God's love very clear in their hearts.

Our judgement of whether or not someone ought to be happy is worth nothing.

Also, happiness comparisons are of no use to anyone and serve no useful purpose.

3.   You're just not praying enough

I can be happy if I have God's peace, right? So all I need to do is pray more and everything will be fine. Conversely, any problems I have are because I'm not praying enough, or I don't have enough faith.

Prayer helps with everything, I firmly believe that. But prayer is best as a two-way conversation, and the kind of prayer that says "Sort this out for me" isn't always going to yield the result you're after. Far better to ask "Show me a different way to look at this", then sit back and wait for an answer to appear.

It can be hard to hear answers to prayers, and the answers aren't always the ones we thought we'd get, and often not the ones we wanted. Asking and listening to the answer are key, I believe, no matter how fervent the prayer, or how long we pray for.

We're all different. We're all born with different challenges to face and we all have different lessons to learn. Just because prayer helps with everything doesn't mean that prayer is the only thing we ever need – sometimes we need each other and sometimes we need the painful lessons before we can really move forward.

If what we're doing isn't working, even if it involves a significant amount of prayer, perhaps we need to try a different approach. Was it Einstein who said insanity is doing the same thing over and over again and expecting different results?

Praying to God for strength is all very well, but what if you have all the strength you need, you just have your foot on the brake, or you've tethered yourself to something that is holding you back?

4.   Can't you just snap out of it

The Beatitudes talks of good to come – you will be comforted, justice will prevail, you will see God, and so on. So what are we all worried about? Shouldn't we just be able to snap out of our negative mindset?

When you feel sad and you talk to someone about it, they might well not be able to relate to your perception of a situation. They might trivialise your concern, or discard your assessment of the situation. They might not agree with your perception of yourself and your ability.

It's not easy to reprogram yourself though. If you've believed something for most of your life, you can't just take someone else's word for it and adjust your mindset. To un-learn something that's affecting your happiness could be a lengthy process and could require a change in thinking habits. It might seem to someone else that you ought to be able to "snap out of it", but to say this to someone caught up with unhelpful thoughts about life or about themselves will only serve to make them feel frustrated or more inadequate.

Thoughts that make us unhappy tend not to be logical. To apply logic to something illogical is like arguing with a drunk person, it'll get you nowhere.

It doesn't matter how many people insist on something being true, unhelpful beliefs can be very hard to shake. If a person is convinced they're unworthy in some way, it doesn't matter how strongly everyone in the world argues that they *are* worthy, they still might not believe it.

5.   I'll be happy when…

Happiness that depends on something happening isn't true happiness. When there's an event you're not looking forward to and you say "I'll be happy when this is over", you're withholding happiness between now and that point – where is the advantage in that?

Likewise, if you want a relationship or a new job, saying "I'll be happy when I've found love", or "when I've got the job" isn't the way it works. In my experience it's when you *are* happy, that you stand a greater chance of finding that relationship, or securing that job. If you start a relationship, job, or anything else, with the intention of having it right every wrong in your life, that's too much pressure and too much expectation. Your unresolved issues might not take centre stage for a while, but there's a good chance they'll be waiting in the wings, ready to reappear when they are least welcome.

Nobody else *makes* you happy. They can allow you to be happy, but the happiness you feel comes from you.

In the same way, nobody else *makes* you sad. They just touch on the trigger points that bring up your underlying sadness.

Applying the formula

If I'm basically a happy person then the Happiness Points might help me to be more happy, but what if I'm desperately unhappy, how can I possibly use the learning points from the Beatitudes to turn my life around?

A more radical approach is to think again about the disciples.

Why can't I be like a disciple?

The disciples were the ones who Jesus was referring to as happy.

They left everything behind, they had to live off the kindness of others, they had no permanent abode, they were to be insulted and ridiculed.

They were happy because they were with Jesus, learning from him, watching him perform miracles, watching him heal people. They could see God working through him and they could experience the peace and joy this brought to all those affected, and to those who were witnesses.

If I want this level of peace, now, today, how do I get it?

I guess I have to see Jesus as more important than anything else in my life. If he was standing here in front of me, in robes and sandals, so that I could touch him, I think I could do that. But he isn't.

What if he was, though? What if he was standing in front of me – would I give up everything and follow him?

I'm not sure I would. I don't know what I have to offer. I'd be worried it'd involve things I'm not very good at – I'm terrified of public speaking and I don't have thick enough skin to put up with being ridiculed.

Ok, so I'm not good enough to be a disciple. Let's hold that thought.

The other question is whether I could walk away from everything I have in my life. I have a husband, children, elderly parents, a dog and a cat. I couldn't leave them.

Why couldn't I leave them?

Why can't I be like a disciple?

Because I love them, because they need me, because I couldn't abandon them.

Perhaps I feel a sense of purpose that comes from looking after others. That's all very well but it doesn't have to be the highest purpose for me. God could have other plans.

Maybe I should understand my attachment to various things. Is it a case of "I have to do this because no-one else will" or "no-one else will do it as well as me"? Somebody else's way could turn out to be a better way, maybe I don't want to entertain that possibility.

This is about my happiness – if I felt my happiness would be improved by walking away from my responsibilities, then is the example of the disciples not giving me permission to do so?

I do know people who left their families behind, well, I can think of only one who left a child behind, but it has been done. In some cultures it's not unusual for grandparents to bring up their grandchildren while parents go off and live a separate life.

I couldn't do it. Even if I thought it would improve my happiness, I couldn't put my happiness above the needs of those around me, it would feel wrong. I couldn't handle the guilt. Even if I thought that in doing so I might achieve my higher purpose.

Then of course there's my job, the fact I need to earn money.

The disciples didn't earn money.

I can't live off thin air.

Why can't I be like a disciple?

The disciples effectively did.

Well I couldn't walk away from financial stability. I wouldn't be happy not knowing where the next meal was coming from. My faith isn't strong enough.

What it all comes down to, then, is: I'm not good enough, I couldn't handle the guilt, and I don't think my faith is strong enough.

Inadequacy and guilt

We're all energetic beings, made up of tiny amounts of matter vibrating at different speeds and with different wavelengths. When we're happy we have a different frequency to when we're sad, or sick. Psychiatrist, physician and spiritual teacher David R Hawkins suggested that our emotions can be mapped according to frequency, with love, joy and peace at the higher levels, and all the negative emotions, such as fear, anger and sadness at the lower levels.

I think of it like driving a car. When you're speeding through life, feeling great joy, you're in the highest gear – fifth or sixth – you put your foot down and fly along. When you're fearful, you might be moving forward, but you'll be going very slowly, perhaps in first gear. When you're angry, you're conflicted and held back, you can't move at a cruising speed. When you're in despair, despondent, depressed, you might not be moving in any direction, you can't find any gear at all.

The lowest frequency emotions are shame and guilt. To me these are both reverse gears. If the objective is to move forward, they're taking us in the wrong direction. Shame, low self-esteem, inadequacy, all would suggest that it's no use starting to move because I'm not good enough, I won't be able to do it. Then I might berate myself for not feeling able to move, hence I go further backwards.

Guilt is similar. Guilt holds me back, it's like a heavy burden that stops me from doing what I want to do. Guilt for something I've done can lead to a general feeling of shame for the person that I am.

We can move up and down through all the emotions in the same day. Some things spark our joy, some things trigger anger and frustration. What's helpful is if we can recognise unhelpful thoughts that lead to negative emotions.

The hardest to understand, I think, are feelings of inadequacy and guilt. Sometimes we might know why we feel this way – we might remember being told we'd never amount to anything, or what we did wasn't right or wasn't good enough – but often we just get so used to feeling inadequate and guilty that we don't even question why.

The turning point, the place we want to get to if we've had negative thoughts, is acceptance. Acceptance of our situation, of the way things are, acceptance of ourselves. Without it we won't be able to move towards happiness.

Acceptance has to be total. It goes hand in hand with forgiveness. If I'm forgiven, perhaps I can forgive myself. If I can forgive myself for something I've done, or for the way I am, perhaps I can accept myself.

I'm not accepting myself if there's a little part of me that I try to deny or disown. If I seek God's peace but hold on to some form of dissatisfaction with part of myself, I'm not going to be able to sustain my uplifted emotions. I need to get acceptance for all of me. God already accepts me, I have to accept me.

True acceptance means no denial, nothing tucked away, hiding in the corners of my mind, no doors closed.

I heard a story once of someone who wanted to devote her life to serving God, and though she wasn't aware of it, she was carrying round guilt for something that had happened in the past. One night she had a vivid dream that gave her a clear reminder of an event that had happened years before, and she realised what she had to do. She had to get forgiveness for something, and forgive herself, despite it being something that would seem to be totally irrelevant to her future life. I think that had she not done this, she would've held herself back in some way, because of her belief in her own guilt.

No harm was done and forgiveness was easy. The hard part had been realising that she'd still been carrying this guilt, when she might not even have been aware of it. The secret she'd been carrying round meant that a door in her mind had been closed. In order to let God's love into every aspect of her life, all doors needed to be open.

I believe that if we don't clear these obstacles to self-love, we're not going to be able to consistently achieve God's peace.

Prayer, Faith and Religion

Anything is better for prayer. Anything. Prayer is part of any answer to any question. But sometimes, the prayer can seem to go unanswered. When this happens it could be that the right prayer is not "Please can this happen" but "Please can you show me what's stopping this from happening?".

"Please can I not feel this low" might be replaced with "Please show me if there's something I've been told that I need to un-learn", or "Please can you show me where my programming needs to change" or "Please show me where I haven't forgiven myself for something".

Prayer is the entreaty to God. Faith enables us to be secure in the knowledge that the prayer will be answered.

What role does religion play?

I'd like to say that religion is the answer, and, of course, it can be. But it can also form part of the problem.

Denominations vary, and individual churches vary, but I'd suggest it has been the case, and to some extent it continues to be, that religion has used guilt. Guilt has been the hook that has encouraged people to church. You must go to church because you're guilty, and the only way to get right with God is for a priest to forgive you, in church.

There will have come a point when church attendances were down and this approach was deemed to be no longer working. Majoring on guilt and God-fearing became unpopular. Church had to be somewhere people wanted to go, or they just wouldn't go.

Or maybe it was simply that church leaders wanted to shift the emphasis to the Love that Jesus spoke of, to the fact that God is Love.

I would suggest, though, that there remains, to a greater or lesser extent, an association between church and guilt, in the eyes of the population at large. Also between church and judgement. Likewise church and gossip.

If you declare yourself to be a Christian, to a non-Christian, it can happen that there's a narrowing of the eyes, a reconsideration of your character, and not in a good way. The expectation is perhaps that you'll be assessing the person you're speaking to, judging them. Perhaps they think you're scoring them against some criteria – do they go to church, do they have any kind of faith, do they drink, smoke, swear?

As I write, in 2022, people are finally emerging from lockdowns and starting to do things that have been forbidden or not advised during the pandemic. It would seem that church attendances have suffered – not necessarily that people aren't partaking in worship in some form, but that they're less likely to attend local services in person.

I feel we're at a cross-roads, in that there's a general decline in attendance and, I would suggest, a massively increased need for the things that church can bring.

We're in the midst of a mental health crisis[6]. Though there are some for whom lockdowns have afforded a reduced, happier pace of life, it would seem there are more who've been negatively impacted by the pandemic in some way. They might have been held in fear for themselves or others, or had financial worries, suffered from isolation, over-work, or lack of work, and so on. All this over a prolonged period.

Fear has infused so much of life. Fear of ill-health or death, fear of causing someone else to be ill, fear of judgement when it becomes clear our attitudes to what constitutes reasonable precautions aren't the same as someone else's.

These things will not help where there has been the kind of unhelpful programming referred to earlier. They take the balance of life in the wrong direction.

If I have deep-rooted feelings of inadequacy then isolation won't help, over-work won't help, financial worry won't help, and any kind of fear simply makes everything worse.

This isn't a political comment on how the pandemic was handled or reported, this is just my view of where we are now, and the problems we are now facing.

If church, whichever denomination, is to help, it has to be able to offer support with regard to mental health.

Part of it, I believe, is to break the link between church and any form of judgement.

I suggest there should be no assessing, weighing up, or even noticing anything that might distinguish us from

---

[6] https://www.mentalhealth.org.uk/our-work/research/coronavirus-mental-health-pandemic

each other. If we seek God's love, that should be enough. Coming together in His name is about what unites us, not what divides us.

Doing or saying anything that could in any way contribute to anyone's feelings of inadequacy or guilt is taking us the wrong way, driving in reverse.

We need each other, that's for sure. Regardless of our differences and any opposing opinions, we need to focus on what we have in common.

What if I were good enough?

The disciples were happy. They had Jesus standing in front of them saying "Come and join me".

If Jesus stood in front of me and said "Come and join me", I imagine one thought would occur to me: Jesus must think I'm good enough.

I'm not perfect. I make mistakes all the time. I'm better at some things than others, some things I'm quite bad at. Sometimes I try hard and get nowhere. Sometimes I don't try hard enough. Sometimes I think I know the right thing to do but I decide not to do it. Sometimes I cut corners. Sometimes I know the choice I'm making is wrong but I do it anyway. Sometimes I just don't have a clue which is the right way. Sometimes I feel it's like I'm playing a board game and nobody's shared with me what the rules of the game are, I'm just making it up as I go along. Sometimes I think I know exactly what a situation needs and I get it totally wrong. All these things are part of being human.

But what if Jesus thinks I'm good enough?

What if Jesus looks at me as he did one of the young fishermen, struggling to catch enough fish? What if he sees beyond my flaws, to a potential I'm not aware of?

What if all Jesus wants from me is for me to say yes?

Perhaps I don't necessarily need to leave my family, job, house, friends and so on. Perhaps I can find God's peace where I am, just as long as I'm willing to look for it.

What if I were good enough?

Maybe, whenever my awareness of my own limitations would have me shrinking back and turning away, or attempting to drive forward with one foot on the brake pedal, I might just have to remind myself that Jesus thinks I'm good enough.

I believe that, with God's help, we're all capable of more than we'll ever know.

I believe that happiness is inevitable if we can let go of feelings of inadequacy, shame and guilt; if we can let go of unforgiveness; if we can replace fear with trust; and if we can be true to ourselves regardless of what others think.

I believe we are good enough.

Appendix: Grammar

With nouns, Greek has the following forms, which can either be singular or plural:

Nominative
- also described as the subject, as in "the <u>dog</u> eats a bone"

Vocative
- which I would use if I were calling my dog "<u>Dog</u>!"

Accusative
- also described as the object, as in "I wash my <u>dog</u>"

Genitive
- which suggests possession, as in "this is my <u>dog's</u> toy"

Dative
- which is usually with a preposition, as in "this has been chewed by the <u>dog</u>"

Adjectives follow the noun they are describing. If I were talking about a black dog, then the word black would follow the above forms, matching the form of the dog it's describing.

"The" follows the above forms, ie it matches the noun it's attached to.

Nouns in Greek are either masculine, feminine or neutral.

Therefore with any adjective or preposition, there are potentially 30 expressions:

> 5 forms, each which can be singular or plural, times 3 genders.

In translating a sentence, or a part of a sentence separated by a link word (for, because etc), we have to first scan the words, looking for the nominative noun and any preposition or adjective that goes with it, then the verb that matches it according to whether it's first/second/third person, singular/plural, then another noun, which could be accusative, genitive or dative, depending on the verb that's used.

Luke 6:21 is an example of a verse where the English words can be translated in the same order as the Greek words:

> Μακάριοι οἱ κλαίοντες νῦν, Ὅτι γελάσετε.
>
> Makarioi hoi klaiontes nyn, hoti gelasete.
>
> Happy (are) the weeping now, for you will laugh.

Whereas the last section of Luke 6:23 is almost back to front:

> κατὰ τὰ αὐτὰ γὰρ ἐποίουν τοῖς προφήταις οἱ πατέρες αὐτῶν.
>
> kata ta auta gar epoioun tois prophetais hoi pateres auton.

In the same way for they treated the prophets the fathers of them.

We know that the fathers are the subject, because the noun for father is nominative (masculine plural). The verb that goes with the fathers (epoioun) is 3rd person plural and goes with a dative (treated), the prophets. The meaning is lost when translated word by word in the correct order.

We get round this sometimes by switching verbs from active to passive "in the same way the prophets were treated by the fathers", which isn't technically correct but effectively gives us the right meaning, whilst still leaving the words in the same order in English as in Greek.

About the Author

Jean Webb studied Ancient Greek at Canon Slade School, Bolton, and then at Birmingham University as part of a combined honours degree in Maths and Ancient Greek, in the late 1980s.

After a career in IT, she now practices as a holistic therapist, and enjoys writing, painting and exploring all aspects of spirituality.

She lives in Oxfordshire with her family.